TAO OF NO STRESS

TAO OF NO STRESS
Three Simple Paths

Stuart Alve Olson

Healing Arts Press
Rochester, Vermont

Healing Arts Press
One Park Street
Rochester, Vermont 05767
www.InnerTraditions.com

Healing Arts Press is a division of Inner Traditions International

*Note to the reader: This book is intended as an informational guide. The remedies,
approaches, and techniques described herein are meant to supplement, and not to be
a substitute for, professional medical care or treatment. They should not be used to treat
a serious ailment without prior consultation with a qualified health care professional.*

Library of Congress Cataloging-in-Publication Data

Olson, Stuart Alve.
  Tao of no stress : three simple paths / Stuart Alve Olson.
    p. cm.
  ISBN-13 : 978-0-89281-987-4
  ISBN-10 : 0-89281-987-1
  1. Stress management. 2. Taoism. I. Title.
  RA785 .O46 2002
  155.9'042—dc21
                        2001006744

Printed and bound in Canada

10 9 8 7 6 5 4 3 2

Text design and layout by Rachel Goldenberg
This book was typeset in Granjon with OptiEve as the display typeface

Contents

THE FIRST PATH
RELEASING STRESS

THE SECOND PATH
MASSAGING STRESS AWAY

THE THIRD PATH
BREATHING STRESS AWAY

Introduction

What Is the Tao of No Stress?

When some of my students first suggested that I write about stress elimination, my immediate reaction was to say no, mostly because I have rarely suffered from the problems of stress, much less made it a focus of my study. But then I realized that my years of Taoist practices had indirectly provided me with numerous practical tools which alleviated the effects of stress. Taoism, at its very core, is about achieving heightened mental and physical states of tranquillity, which can be very useful to the modern-day sufferer of stress.

I have spent over twenty-five years studying, learning, writing about, and teaching the daily disciplines of how to deepen one's state of relaxation and let go of physical and mental tension and anxiety; that is, how to let go of stress. I didn't consciously set out to learn how to stop suffering from stress; rather, I intended to learn how to achieve tranquillity and relaxation of body and mind through the practices of t'ai chi, qigong, massage, and meditation. My practices just happened to create the conditions that eliminated the effects of stress.

Early in my life I was fortunate enough to have studied teachings and practices that showed me how to yield, accept, and remain calm in the worst of situations, so suffering the negative effects of stress hasn't been a factor in my life. I am by no means claiming that my life is trouble free, but I have learned how not to pile the additional, negative effects of stress onto whatever difficulties I am experiencing.

There is a familiar saying that warns never to ask people who aren't rich how to get rich; if they knew, wouldn't they already be rich? In Taoism, no student would ever seek to learn from a teacher who had not achieved high levels of tranquillity. No martial arts student would attempt to learn from a teacher who had no martial skills. The same applies in finding out how to eliminate stress. If you want to know how to eliminate stress, ask someone who is without stress.

Taoist teachings, from which the material in this book is drawn, contain wonderfully practical methods and advice for eliminating stress. The success of these practices can be witnessed in the long lives of great Taoist masters. Moreover, the methods presented in this book are a distillation of the past twenty-five years of my own experience. I can tell you that they have worked for me and I am confident they will prove accessible and useful for anyone.

WHAT IS STRESS?

Stress is by definition the sum of biological reactions to adverse stimuli that disturb or interfere with the homeostasis of an organism and result in emotional or physical strain or tension. The adverse stimuli can be either internal or external, and it is the person's reaction to them that can lead to illness or disease. Although every person has the capacity to adjust physically or emotionally to adverse stimuli in his or her life, many people don't know how to make use of this capacity, and consequently suffer from stress.

TYPES OF STRESS

There are two types of stress: alarm and continued. These are more commonly known as acute and chronic stress, respectively. I use the terms *alarm* and *continued* for clarity because they are more reflective of the actual qualities of each type of stress.

Alarm stress refers to the response to an immediate physical threat. The medullas of your adrenal glands cause the release of the hormone epinephrine into your bloodstream. Your heart rate then increases, blood pressure rises, and the blood vessels dilate, which in turn decreases your blood sugar supply and dilates the pupils of your eyes. During alarm stress, the breath moves high up into your chest, your muscles feel cold, and your body undergoes what is called a protective response.

Alarm stress is rarely injurious, but, if the adrenals become too exhausted, the result can be fatal. This type of stress results from either a real threat or a falsely perceived one.

Continued stress is far more complex and dangerous, as it gradually weakens the adrenal glands, which in turn can adversely affect the heart, blood, and nervous system. When this happens, a wide range of ailments can ensue. The effects of continued stress can be experienced in three basic degrees: *sporadic, chronic,* and *acute*.

- *Sporadic* continued stress refers to periodic times in a person's life when he or she is under the strain— real or perceived—of a particular situation, and it usually disappears when the situation resolves itself.

The situation need not be negative, as even positive emotions and experiences can create stress, such as falling in love, receiving an award, buying a new car, and so on. Normally, only minor illnesses result from this type of stress effect.

- *Chronic* continued stress is much more serious, as it is a habitual reaction to almost all of life's experiences. This chronic effect creates very serious health ailments, such as high blood pressure, heart attack, cancer, and a variety of other serious illnesses and diseases.

- The *acute* form of continued stress is the most serious, as it causes a complete shutdown of psychological equilibrium, which is sometimes referred to as a nervous breakdown. This effect of continued stress is the most difficult to cure and can cause irreparable damage to both the central nervous system and the immune system.

THEORIES OF STRESS

Western medicine has accepted the correlation between stress and illness, but does not outright claim that all forms of stress create an illness or ill effect. In Western medicine, the apparent root cause of an illness is diagnosed based strictly on the symptoms of the illness. Taoism asserts that *all* stresses and anxieties have a physical and mental effect on the person, and that in the end all our illnesses have their source in negative mental actions or thoughts. Western skepticism can be partially justified, in that stress can affect a person either negatively or positively. Since all stress stimulates the adrenal glands, stress can sometimes create the capacity for individuals to perform wondrous physical feats. In certain individuals, stress can provide motivation for great accomplishments. The majority who experience stress, however, do so in a negative way. It may be the case that stress stimulates a positive response in people who have an increased supply of adrenal hormones. Inversely, those who react to stress in a negative manner have a decreased supply.

To the Taoist, however, this whole matter of how a person reacts to stress is purely a question of positive *qi*—the internal energy that all Taoists aspire to experience flowing through their body—or negative *qi*. In more specific terms a person is endowed with either good or poor "inherited *qi*" and "self-acquired *qi*." The Taoists term these as: "before heaven *qi*," the mental and physical energy received from one's parents; and "after heaven *qi*," the energy a person accumulates from his or her own efforts. If a person's *qi* is strong and abundant, the Taoist believes that the quality, vitality, and length of his or her life will be greatly increased.

Qi is not hormonal; rather it is what affects and stimulates hormones. In a sense, *qi* is like a latent oxygen in the blood that can promote increased health and stamina. Ultimately, it is the energy that animates a human being, the unseen power source that mobilizes all physical and mental functions of the body. In Chinese, *qi* means both vital life energy and breath, as it is the breath that either accumulates or dissipates *qi*. Proper breathing accumulates it; poor breathing dissipates it.

Stress dissipates *qi* because the breathing is obstructed; thus a person's health and longevity are adversely affected. Acupuncture, developed by early Taoists, in its essence is a means whereby *qi* is balanced, which results in a regularizing of all the body's functions.

Western medicine is gradually making progress toward the acceptance of the validity of acupuncture and *qi*. The gradual acceptance is owing mostly to the incredible cures witnessed by many Western medical practitioners. Still, Western medicine is hesitant to accept Eastern explanations for the cures that come from balancing and restoring *qi*.

Nevertheless, both Western and Eastern health practices agree that stress is not only unwanted and injurious but also that relaxation and breathing play an important role in eliminating it. Western medicine, however, is still confused about *how* to eliminate stress; Eastern practice is not.

In recent years more studies have appeared in the West that highly recommend Asian methods for healing. The main reason for the high praise is that the studies have found that such methods not only greatly increase blood circulation but also strengthen the immune system and central equilibrium (a person's sense of balance).

People who suffer from stress normally experience poor blood circulation and loss of balance. Any medical doctor will tell you that if you increase your blood circulation, you will alleviate numerous health problems, from arthritis to migraine headaches. When there is poor blood circulation the body's immune system cannot function properly. If the immune system malfunctions, then the body is completely open to numerous diseases, ranging from the common cold to cancer. Stress is the number one cause of poor blood circulation.

Many people believe that stress can be cured simply by resting or relaxing, but this is true only of very minor types of stress. Resting, or doing nothing, is purely a short-term means to releasing minor anxieties and avoiding taking more stress into the body. Rest is fine for relieving tension or creating a calm mind for making an important decision, but it really has nothing to do with curing stress. Rest can actually just hide stress that would be revealed if, for example, you were to undergo a treadmill stress test. Once stress is present in the body, inaction will not cure it. When left unattended, this stress will show up in your dreams, hobbies, relationships, and work.

As explained in more detail later, stress is a self-trained response. If you want to eliminate it and its harmful effects from your life, rather than trying to suppress or avoid it, you must learn to change your response to the things that create stress. Changing your mental response requires changing your physical state or activity. There is no such thing as thinking your way out of stress, so if you want to change the responses in your mind, you must first make changes in your body. Altering the stress response is accomplished by incorporating the three basic physical functions of *releasing, massaging,* and *breathing.* Methods for how to do this are provided in the three corresponding sections of this book.

THE TAO OF NO STRESS

A central theme of Taoism is "active nonaction" (in Chinese, *wei wu wei*), abiding by noninterference, nonaggression, and noncontention. Active nonaction is a positive way of living in accord with nature and the self. Our lives become stressed because we are constantly "actively in action," forcing our way through life's conditions and experiences, so much so that the *activity* is seen as more important than the *doer* of the actions. When, however, we lose the desire to interfere, to be aggressive, and to contend, peace and tranquillity infuse us, and so we emulate active nonaction.

Taoism does not speak to the masses but to the individual. It is not concerned with how to be worldly but how to be "naturally just so," as the great Taoist philosopher Chuang-tzu expressed it. Stress comes from too much attachment to worldly affairs and concerns and not enough love for the well-being of the self. Everything we do is a reflection of what is going on inside ourselves, and when we are too much attached to worldly concerns, we not only create stress but we also pass it on to others and out into the world. When the self is content with itself, problems and stresses cease.

My Taoist teacher loved to say, "Health is of the utmost importance; everything else is secondary." This means that focusing on your health and well-being will in the end take care of everything else in your life. Being healthy, being alive, being content, being "naturally just so": the concept is so simple that it is easily overlooked. It is from these Taoist ideals that I have formed the basis of this work for the elimination of stress. I can see no other solution or cure to the pressures and stresses of the world except to make efforts toward health, living, and contentment, just as the Taoists of old exemplified with their own lives.

WHAT IS STRESS ELIMINATION?

Understanding why stress afflicts you, as well as how to completely eliminate it, is absolutely crucial to living a longer and healthier life. Therefore, in discussing how to eliminate stress, I don't talk of reducing, managing, or controlling it—such words imply that stress is something you have to hold on to, as if it were a necessary part of you. Would you prefer to reduce heart attacks, or eliminate them? I think the answer is obvious. So why would anyone want to waste time and energy reducing, managing, or controlling stress? Wouldn't it be better just to eliminate it?

Stress—though not an illness itself—becomes the door through which illness and disease walk freely into our bodies. Allowing stress into your life is akin to asking illness and disease to come and live in your body. Would you rather reduce cancer, or eliminate it? An old Taoist text says, "People do not meet with undeserved suffering and misfortune; rather they invite them into themselves." When we eliminate stress, we shut the door to poor physical and mental health.

As I mentioned earlier, altering the mental response that induces stress requires making changes in your body, and the three paths toward this physical change are *releasing, massaging,* and *breathing.* Each of the three paths is, in turn, divided into two parts: *theory* and *method.* Because "theory without practice is sterile; practice without theory is blind," I do not intend to provide here methods for eliminating stress without giving an explanation as to why they are effective.

The basis for the material presented in this book dates far back to the early Taoists, China's first naturalists. Since their teachings are ancient, you might ask why they are being presented to modern-day sufferers of stress. The answer is simple: they work!

Originally intended and developed for Taoists who sought to acquire tranquillity of body and mind, these teachings enabled practitioners to rid themselves of even the faintest trace of tension, anxiety, and stress. If taken to their ultimate end, these teachings would do much more than rid a person of stress. With the more modest goal in mind, however, the simple methods presented in this book should prove to be very effective and efficient in eliminating your stress.

Even though the theories and methods provided here are divided into three parts, they should be approached as a whole. The principles and actions of *breathing, releasing,* and *massaging* are all crucial to each other, so it is important to understand all three paths before applying any of the methods.

THE THREE PATHS TO ELIMINATING STRESS

At the heart of Taoist teachings we find three basic and important criteria for eliminating stress. The first is to acquire a mind-set that allows for the release of your self-trained responses to stressful situations. As you begin to pay attention to releasing stress, it should become clear that responses to stress are often habitual. Take, for example, people who experience degrees of road rage every time they drive. The stress will manifest itself on the road, but it often relates more to some other problem in their life than it does to their actual driving experience. In Taoism it is thought that a person is not necessarily violent simply because he hates someone else—it is because there is something in himself he hates, and his violent actions are but an external venting of his own inner turmoil. Unfortunately, habitual responses to stress, such as road rage or violence, often create further causes for stress. Identifying your self-trained responses to stress—and acquiring a mind-set that immediately recognizes and releases these responses—is the first step in becoming stress free.

The second criterion is to learn how to pay attention to yourself in a positive manner rather than a negative manner in which you focus on only the negative effects of your experience of being stressed. This process is very simple, as it is accomplished by massaging and pressing certain areas of the body to alleviate the negative physical effects of stress. These massaging methods alter the central nervous system's impulses for reacting to stress and train it to respond in a way that eliminates stress.

For example, if you are one of those people who experience frequent bouts with road rage, the cure is first to release the rage, to let it go. Then pull over and utilize both the massaging and breathing techniques to release the stress. Over time this will create a self-trained positive response when you are experiencing road rage or any other stress.

The third criterion is to learn how to breathe stress away. Breathing is the most important bodily function we have; it directly affects the circulation of the blood and our central nervous system. In Taoist spiritual cultivation nothing plays a bigger role than the discipline and practice of breathing methods. The Chinese term *qi* translates simultaneously as both "breath" and "vital-life energy." *Qi* is the animator of life, for without it the body is lifeless. When the *qi* is low in the abdomen the body and mind are tranquil. When the *qi* is high in the chest the body and mind are agitated. Therefore, based on the Taoist concept of *qi,* the elimination of stress relies greatly on our ability to breathe correctly.

THE FIRST PATH

RELEASING STRESS

The Theory of Releasing Stress

THE MEANING OF RELEASING

First of all, no one can make stress leave his or her body, just as you cannot make your body relax or make your mind be calm. You have to *let* your body relax and your mind become calm. In the same manner, you must *let* stress leave your body.

If you took a glass of water and put some debris inside with the purpose of getting all the debris to the bottom of the glass, would it be easier to take a spoon and push all the debris down, or to just let the debris sink to the bottom of the glass of its own accord? Obviously, if you try to push the debris down with a spoon, the debris will never settle at the bottom of the glass because you're constantly agitating the water. And yet, by simply letting the glass sit still, the debris will automatically sink to the bottom of the glass.

This analogy of debris in water reveals the secret to the elimination of stress in our lives: we have to learn how to let stress go of its own accord. Stress can become habitual and even addictive to people who simply haven't learned to let go of it. People who hold onto stress, thinking they will let it go once they've gotten through certain difficulties or stressful events in their lives, are like water-skiers who fall and continue to hang onto the rope, only to be dragged through the water. And as they wait for the boat to slow down (or for life to become less stressful) their bodies incur damage. It's obvious that letting go is the smart thing to do, so why do the majority of us hang onto it?

Releasing stress is not the same as avoiding the problem or situation that created the stress. Releasing is an active process of engaging the problem by not only performing methods for physically releasing stress, but also changing your mental attitude from that of wanting to hold onto stress to wanting to let go of it. In desiring to learn how to release your stress, you are telling yourself that you are more important than the problem or situation you are experiencing. Through the act of releasing, you empower yourself to resolve the problem in an efficient, stress-free manner.

One of the sad facts about human nature is that we normally don't, or can't, change our lives unless we have to. A situation often has to become critical before we can turn our lives around. As you learn to release stress, your habitual behaviors will confront you time and time again. Unless you have no choice but to change, you will more than likely fall back into your old, established patterns.

The Taoists believe that for people to successfully make changes, they have to in essence trick themselves so as not to activate their habitual, negative behaviors. This theory of tricking yourself to make a change is really ingenious, and it relies on the repetition of certain behaviors and the replacement of others.

For example, consciously saying to yourself, "I want to move around," rather than telling yourself, "I have to exercise," makes a huge difference in how the mind responds to—and how you act upon—the idea. Like birds that fly every day because it's their nature to do so, human beings need to move every day because it's their nature to do so. Birds don't stop flying because they have something better to do or want to take a day off. Likewise, human beings shouldn't go a whole day without moving; we can't have good health unless we move every day. Call this movement "exercise" if you wish, but the very word exercise can cause resistance in people who feel they aren't doing it enough or that they should be more disciplined in performing it. "Discipline" can be another stress-filled term. Language is very important to consider when you think about changing your behavior and thought patterns. It is better to think that you will move every day because it is your nature to move every day; the basis of all exercise is simply movement anyway. Often when we *want* to do something we will, but when we think we *have* to, we usually reject it. You trick yourself into changing physically by using physical movement, and you trick yourself mentally by the way you think about that movement.

The methods provided in this book should be used every day, but only when you feel like it and time permits. Don't schedule these activities, because if you do, your mind will consider them as disciplined exercises and will resist your best intentions.

The secret here lies in the difference between repetition and discipline. Simply doing something every day is not the same as disciplining yourself to do something every day, and the problem is that most people believe that if they discipline themselves to do something, they will be successful in creating change. Unfortunately, this is rarely true. More often than not they are initially very enthusiastic about their new activity or change in their behavior, but gradually their enthusiasm dies off, and, like dieters who go off a diet and gradually gain the lost weight back, they find the behavior change and its results are not lasting. They fail because they tried to force a change. Change in what and when to eat comes about not from disciplining oneself in a particular diet, but from simply repeating every day a different pattern.

Just as it is very difficult to add a new, positive behavior to your life, such as sticking to a certain diet, it is equally difficult to stop performing a habitual, negative behavior, such as hanging onto your stress. Replacing your undesirable behavior with a desirable one, however, makes it easier.

Smokers find it difficult to stop their smoking until they discover something to fill the vacuum in their behavior that would otherwise be occupied with the act and thoughts of smoking. It is not enough to simply tell yourself that you will quit a negative behavior without finding something positive with which to replace it. The release of stress requires the same procedure.

The trick is to simply perform the techniques given here, but with no more goal or thought than just feeling good when you do them. When you do so in a repetitive manner over a period of time, you will find that your body will gradually want more and more of that good feeling, and just as with stress, alcohol, or drugs, the body becomes addicted; the old habit of accumulating stress will thus be replaced by a new one of eliminating it. Keep in mind that your responses to stress were not created in one day; they took time to develop. No one becomes a stress addict (or an alcoholic or drug addict, gambler, or sex addict) in one day. You train your body to like what you do to it, whether it is good or bad for your health. Stress responses come from behavioral habits deeply embedded through years of training.

When following the methods, never tell yourself that more is better; just do a little each day when it is convenient. Otherwise you will be telling your body memory and intelligence that there is reason to resist a change, and they will. Addictions and habits develop a memory and intelligence of their own. The methods of cure must also acquire an intelligence and consciousness of their own. This premise is precisely where Eastern and Western medicine separate, but anyone who has suffered habitual stress or addictions knows that their energy is very difficult to change.

The Taoist personifies everything, believing that negative habits and addictions are like children, or like spirits and demons, who must be distracted by something in order to stop their negative behavior. An analogy can be made to a child playing in a burning house. If you yell out to him to run out of the house, you will most likely only cause him to panic and remain inside frozen in terror. But if you simply offer him a new toy and calmly suggest that he can have it if he just walks out to get it, he will likely do so, safely. When people are no longer controlled by their negative behavior, represented by the burning house, they can see how destructive it really was. Stress is your child in many respects, and to panic yourself into coaxing it out will only create more stress and injury—it is far better to give stress a good reason for leaving of its own accord.

So, knowing how to release stress is crucial, and, toward that end, an understanding of some of the primary causes of stress and how to change self-trained stress responses is important. Like the fallen water-skier and the child in the burning house, you have to learn how to become calm and let go of panic or anxiety in order to get to safety.

CHANGING YOUR SELF-TRAINED STRESS RESPONSES

Stress, generally speaking, is actually nothing more than a self-trained response we have developed in dealing with problems and uncomfortable situations. Getting rid of stress can be quick and easy, but only if we allow ourselves to change the response. Changing a behavior or trained response, however, is very difficult for most of us. A Japanese monk once said in regards to people repeating the same mistakes in life, "When a person keeps walking into the same wall, he will usually do it over and over again. It becomes his Zen." Just as we tend to keep pointlessly repeating the same mistake throughout life (despite the ignorance and uselessness of repeatedly walking into a wall), we also tend to repeat the trained response of stress.

Stress is learned. We learn it from parents, brothers and sisters, friends, society, even from actors in movies and on television—but ultimately, we must accept the fact that we give it to ourselves; we allow it into our lives. But if we allow it in, we can likewise let it go out.

We live in a busy, fast-paced world, and many people who feel the need to keep up also think they need to appear stressed out so that others around them will think they are working hard—all to create a picture of being busy or successful. Stress has become in many ways a badge of honor, just as facial sword scars were a sign of bravery for Prussian soldiers. Unlike battle scars, however, stress is purely self-inflicted.

Many of us keep making the same mistakes over and over again in life, not because we want to but because we don't recognize the need for change until a situation becomes extreme. An alcoholic or drug addict usually doesn't see the need to quit until all is lost. The stress addict, too, doesn't normally change until illness forces her to. "To remove a mountain is easy, but to change a person's temperament is much more difficult," so the old Chinese adage goes. To eliminate stress before it creates an illness is difficult for most people because it involves change. Even though we can feel the effects of stress in our body, our mind does not seek ways of eliminating stress. The trained response of feeling stress has become normal to the body. Perceived as normal, stress becomes part of our everyday life. Sensing stress, we might decide to take a vacation or do some relaxing activity to calm the stress, but we don't change the cause. The body uses illness to warn us that there is unchecked stress, but our awareness is usually of the illness, not of the underlying stress, its cause, and so we treat the illness and not the stress itself. An example of the tendency is writing with a pencil and pressing so hard that the lead breaks, then cursing the weakness of the pencil point and overlooking the extreme pressure that is the real cause of the breakage: blame the tension in your hand and let it go.

I don't pretend to offer a recipe for living a perfect life, free from all stress; no one can do that. Indeed, stress can sometimes get us to do things or take care of problems we have long avoided. This type of stress leaves once the task has been accomplished, so this is a sort of stress that can be useful. The type of stress this book focuses on, however, is the kind of chronic stress, the trained response, that creates numerous health problems and is best eliminated.

There are many causes of stress. Most Westerners can trace the majority of their stress to problems with money, love, or sex. Why? Because we become attached to things in our lives, and when we perceive that attachment is threatened, we commonly experience a stress response. Money as a cause of stress represents our attachment to material things; love, attachment to our emotions; and sex, attachment to our deepest self, or the need to express ourselves physically and emotionally to connect to another.

It's important to remember that stress is a perception, a self-trained response to an incident or situation that appears difficult or threatening. Learning how to change the perception changes the response, and so eliminates the stress. Money, love, and sex are not the problems; rather, the stress we experience in relation to them arises from our perceptions of our relationship to them. We usually prefer to locate the source of our discomfort somewhere outside of us. The reality is that the source of the stress response is always something inside us. We rarely view the stress response as the problem; rather we see it only as a negative effect of something else causing us to feel stress. I learned this many years ago while

I was listening to a psychologist on the radio who was discussing cures for stress. He made a statement that seemed very disturbing to me: "If I could give each of my clients five thousand dollars, I would eliminate their stress. Not having enough money is more often than not my clients' root problem." This is a very sad statement, not only about our culture and times but also about an individual's priorities. I disagree wholeheartedly with this psychologist's solution. Is money really the root of all evil or is our relationship to it at the root of our stress? In the majority of cases, lack of money is not the problem, lack of contentment is. I've known many incredibly rich people, and they have as much stress as, if not more than, anyone else.

I witnessed this phenomenon with an old acquaintance, a man who made millions of dollars selling luxury yachts. One day while eating lunch with him, I jokingly asked him what it felt like to be a multimillionaire. He answered me in a way I didn't expect: "Earning the money was fun and easy, trying to keep it is what's killing me." He was suffering from ulcers, high blood pressure, and had recently experienced a mild stroke. Money certainly did not guarantee his physical or mental health.

The majority of us need to make money, as our culture and times demand that we do. But what is more important, our health or wealth? Obviously, without good health we can never enjoy our wealth. Many people put their lives in the ironic situation of working really hard to attain financial security, only to spend their hard-earned money on repairing the damage they have done to their health. We are too busy earning a living to actually live. We might do well to take to heart Benjamin Franklin's advice: "Early to bed, early to rise makes a man healthy, wealthy, and wise." This statement has such a profoundly Taoist sensibility to me that, if I didn't know its author, I would be convinced a Taoist wrote it.

Without good health we simply cannot enjoy life, no matter how much money we have. It is obvious, then, that we must learn how to take care of ourselves. We can approach health maintenance in one of two manners: we can treat our bodies like a car, having it fixed only when it breaks down; or we can treat it like a garden, daily tending and nurturing it so everything grows strong. The first approach is "curative maintenance," and the second is "preventative maintenance." Prevention is of course far preferable and a lot less costly.

We as a society have grown ever more reliant on the diagnosis and cures of doctors and much less so on our own efforts to stay healthy. Thomas Edison is reported to have once said in an interview, "All medicine will eventually become holistic." He clearly saw long ago the eventual negative outcome of our reliance on drugs and surgery to keep us healthy. It might be well for us to look at how the ancient Taoists, those hermits who sought to free themselves of all worldly concerns and stresses, approached this subject of stress elimination:

Hearing the sound of flowing water calms the ear.
Seeing the green of trees and plants calms the eye.
Eating food that is fresh calms the stomach.
Smelling the odors of nature calms the senses.
Touching things soft and delicate calms the nerves.

Walk with a staff in natural places;
feel the breath low in the abdomen;
sit with no concern for the world;
live like the wind blowing over the earth.

All then is free and easy, and even if a mountain
fell at your feet, you would give it no notice.

Although the verse's advice was meant for those who sought to free themselves from the bondage of worldly affairs, there is much we who live in the modern world can learn from these words.

Those of us who are modern city dwellers might listen to a water fountain, go to a garden or park, eat fruits or vegetables in season, smell some flowers, hold a child, take a walk around a lake, close the door, shut off the phone, breathe deep, and relax for a while. In short, we might begin perceiving the good things about our life and embracing those things that make us feel better and that are important to us.

When we look closely at this advice, it is not necessarily just about getting rid of stress but more about paying attention to our self and not to the problems in our life. At some point in our lives, we all need to ask ourselves, "What is more important, me or the problem?" If you take care of the *me,* the problem will be much easier to solve. But if you focus on only the problem, the *me* only gets worse. All of us, whether suffering from stress or not, need to devote some portion of our day to just the *me.* When we do, life miraculously improves and is far more enjoyable.

The methods provided in this book go well beyond simply preventing and eliminating the stress response. They help remove the effects of stress as well. When a person is suffering from a stress-induced headache, it is not enough to point out that stress is the cause of the headache and suggest ways to avoid the stress; it is necessary to recommend a cure for the headache as well. So this book is especially designed to provide cures and preventive steps for ailments most commonly associated with stress.

Many years ago I read a passage in an old Taoist manual that really impressed me. It stated: "No one ever need suffer from an illness, as health is nature's gift to man. It is man who fritters away this gift through lack of being aware of his own self." Pay attention to yourself, take time for yourself, and be yourself. It sounds simple, and it is. Unfortunately, many people give all their attention to their problems, take all their time for their problems, and ultimately become their problems. My hope is the following pages will help you avoid that.

The Methods of Releasing Stress

THERAPY OF SIX SOUNDS

Although sound therapy has gained acceptance in Western medicine only recently, it has been part of Eastern health practices for centuries. One of the most effective systems for using sound was developed in the fifth century A.D. by the famous Taoist physician T'ao Hung-ching. T'ao discovered that vocalizing different sounds while expelling the breath could cleanse and restore the organs, regulate the blood circulatory system, and stabilize the central nervous system.

T'ao's Six Sounds practice should not seem so far-fetched, since expelling air and making sound are two functions the body naturally uses to ward off stress. When people are under stress, they will naturally sigh, moan, or blow out air. These constitute the body's natural release of built-up stress. We also know that certain music or sounds can alter emotions and influence physical activity. Sound as part of the Lamaze method for childbirth has proven very effective, and primal screaming methods have been shown to be beneficial for the release of anger, for example.

Discovering that human beings naturally expel air and make sounds to feel better, T'ao determined which sounds had the greatest effect in stimulating the body's natural functions. T'ao discovered there are basically six syllables that create positive vibrations in specific regions of the body and thus stimulate the natural healing responses of the body. The sixth syllable is of the greatest importance to the sufferer of stress, as it is specifically intended for the release of stress, anxiety, and tension. All the syllables should be used daily, however, to help stabilize the body and maintain good health.

METHOD

The production of the Six Sounds should be done according to the following general method. Sit comfortably on the edge of a chair with your spine erect and your head held upright. Place your feet flat on the floor with the knees slightly apart and rest the palms of your hands on your thighs. Make all your inhalations through the nose and direct your breath into the lower abdomen. Expand the lower abdomen while inhaling and contract it when exhaling, so that the breath completely leaves the body. The exhalation should be much longer than the inhalation. When exhaling a sound, do so from the lower abdomen, not from the throat.

Although the inhalation through the nose remains the same for each of the six different sounds, the manner of exhalation differs for each, and the instructions and effects for each sound are provided below. After inhaling and expelling a sound, breathe normally through the nose for a couple of breaths before making the sound again; this will avoid making your breathing erratic or agitated.

Repeat each syllable six times.

1. Shoo

Making the sound *shoo* alleviates problems associated with a sense of malaise. The vibration of this sound positively affects the liver and gall bladder.

Purse the lips and make the sound *shoo* for the length of the exhalation. The jaw should be slightly open and your tongue curled slightly upward.

2. Haa

Making the sound *haa* alleviates anger. The vibration of this sound calms the heart and regulates the small intestine.

Open the mouth wide and generate the sound *haa*. The tip of the tongue is held lightly against the inside of the lower teeth.

3. Hoo

Making the sound *hoo* regulates the lungs, and eradicates any impurities brought in by the breath. It can also help regulate body temperature. The vibration of this sound balances the spleen, pancreas, and stomach.

Purse the lips and make the sound *hoo*. The jaw should be slightly open and the tongue curled slightly downward.

4. Sss

Making the sound *sss* helps to regain equilibrium in the nervous system and body generally. The vibration of this sound cleanses the lungs and regulates the large intestine.

With the upper and lower teeth held gently together and the tongue placed directly behind the teeth, draw the lips back and make the sound *sss*.

5. Foo

Making the sound *foo* regulates body temperature so the body does not become either too hot or too cold. The vibration of this sound stabilizes the kidneys, bladder, and adrenal glands.

Purse the lips and make the sound *foo*. The jaw should be slightly open and the tongue drawn slightly back and up towards the roof of the mouth.

6. Shee

Making the sound *shee* relieves stress, tension, and anxiety. The vibration of this sound regulates the blood circulatory system and the central nervous system. If you are under stress, the sounding of this syllable should be performed thirty-six times.

With the upper and lower teeth held gently together and the tongue pressing lightly against the upper teeth, draw the lips back and make the sound *shee*.

THERAPY OF THE CAT'S WALK

Taking a walk, especially out in nature, among trees, can release a great deal of stress. Taoists developed very specific techniques for walking as a method to improve health. Because they considered cats, especially the tiger, to be the most adept walkers, they developed a practice which they referred to as "walking like a cat."

Walking has been proven to be the best relief for the effects of osteoarthritis, which almost anyone over the age of sixty suffers from to one degree or another. Walking improves blood circulation, helps maintain a healthy weight, tightens and thickens ligaments, keeps joints well lubricated, supplies oxygen to the entire body, and regulates elimination of body wastes.

Studies on walking have shown that thirty minutes of daily walking can raise HDL (High Density Lipoprotein—commonly known as the "good" cholesterol) levels, and for people with diabetes, walking improves blood glucose control and decreases insulin resistance.

Walking is one of the best and safest exercises a person can perform, but sadly most Americans walk only to and from their car. We need to take more time for walking, as the benefits of it are so great.

METHOD

As you walk, place your heel on the ground and then roll the rest of the foot down. You are not in a race, so walk slowly. Keep the breath low in the abdomen, breathing in through your nose and exhaling through your mouth. Above all, keep your breath natural. Don't try to slow it down or make it deeper than what it naturally is. Just keep your attention on your lower abdomen and your breath will take care of itself.

Like a cat, swivel your head periodically as if looking around while you walk; turn your head in this manner every ten steps or so.

Use a walking stick whenever possible. The Taoists felt that walking with a staff would keep their arms from waving around, which can hinder relaxation and cause the breath to rise into the lungs rather than sink into the abdomen.

Go barefoot when possible. Walking barefoot on grass or at the beach really increases your energy and good spirits. Shoes prevent us from feeling the earth and obstruct the natural stimulation of energy in the feet.

Do not make walking a discipline or practice; rather, consider it a means for just feeling good. Let your body get addicted to it.

My teacher once told me, "If you live within three blocks of a store, never drive there, walk. Gradually you will become addicted to it. Not only will you spend less money because you won't want to carry so much back with you, you will lose weight because of the walking and buy fewer useless food items."

His advice was so simple I almost passed it by. It was amazing to witness how many excuses I initially made for not following it. I invite you to attempt this simple practice, observing your own initial response. When he told me this, he was eighty-five years old and walked to the grocery store every day.

THE SECOND PATH

MASSAGING STRESS AWAY

3

The Theory of Massaging Stress Away

In the preceding sections of the book I have described the nature of stress and the efficacy of making certain sounds and walking for releasing stress and enhancing overall health; in this section I concentrate on the theory and methods of massaging stress away.

Massage has long been a staple of Chinese medicine, and recently it has been growing in popularity within the Western medical community. Therapeutic touch, as it is popularly referred to, has in the past several years been introduced into many hospitals across the United States. In essence, touching the body by either rubbing, pressing, or squeezing greatly helps rid it of stress, primarily because these massage techniques increase the blood circulation, which sends fresh supplies of blood to the muscles and organs of the body and thus enhances their health and vigor.

One of the most interesting observations I have made about Asian culture is the presence of an open and healthy perception of massage, both self-massage and massage by another person. This perception is one we in the West will hopefully continue to embrace, as all forms of massage are very beneficial to our overall physical health, and especially for regulating and calming the entire central nervous system.

Asians accept massage as being both healthy and normal, and I have often been struck by how members of an Asian family will often massage each other's feet, hands, or necks while watching television, for example, or just sitting around talking. Maybe this custom is one of the reasons Asians have the lowest incidence of stress-related illnesses. Members of Western families, on the other hand, normally do not engage in such activity and, further, may tend to separate themselves in such situations.

While massage is gaining acceptance in the medical community, a good portion of Western society still considers massage as a sexual activity, preventing us from experiencing its benefits in other areas of our lives. Everything from a friendly pat on the back to an affectionate embrace signals your nervous system that others accept and care for you. Just as babies and infants respond to being touched and held by their parents and others, adults understand friendly touching as a sign that they are loved. Westerners, however, are sometimes disturbed when people outside their sphere of familiar contact attempt to express their emotions or feelings through touch.

Touching is a basic need in all human beings. Without it, we lose our sense of belonging, of being loved, and of well-being in general. We measure the depth of our relationships through touch. Whether through sex or a handshake, touch tells us many things about ourselves and others.

Stress, more than any other affliction, causes us to reject or withdraw from physical contact with others. We tend to shun it because it creates yet another emotion or stimulus that we consider too difficult or undesirable to deal with at the time. When we are under stress, however, physical contact with another or self-massage can greatly reduce its effects.

For our purposes here, the methods discussed will pertain solely to self-massage techniques, not massage by another person. This type of massage is highly recommended for everyone, stressed or not.

The Chinese equivalent for *massage* is literally "dry bathing"; another term is *tui na,* which refers primarily to acupressure, similar to the Japanese art of shiatsu, which is a constellation of methods of pressing and rubbing on specific points in the body to generate energy and blood flow. These methods form the basis of the techniques discussed in the next chapter.

The concept of *relaxing (sung)* in Chinese health techniques has fascinating connection with the elimination of stress. Whereas the Western notion of relaxation generally means completely letting go, doing absolutely nothing, and even sleeping, the Chinese term implies alertness, attentiveness, and sensitivity. The idea is that unless we stay alert to stress, pay attention to it, and develop a sensitivity toward it, we will not be able to prevent or eliminate it.

The Chinese understanding is well illustrated by the physical and mental state of a cat. Even when a cat sleeps soundly, it remains totally aware of its environment. Given the slightest alteration in its environment, like the sudden rustling of a mouse, the cat will instantly react. A cat's capacity to stay both relaxed and alert combines with the cat's physiology to give it unique abilities: it can fall from a great height unscathed; it can move and bend with great flexibility; it can jump a distance of ten times its height; and it can bound at great speed from a stationary position. In order to achieve these things, it is necessary for the cat to maintain a relaxed but alert state. It is little wonder that martial arts in China often incorporated the special characteristics of the cat.

Elimination of stress, therefore, is most effectively achieved not by simply lying down and falling asleep, since the stress response and its effects will only lie dormant and awaken again when you encounter another stressful situation. Rather, the idea is to do something about stress, to be alert, attentive, and sensitive to it.

Once when I was learning how to sit in meditation, a monk advised me on how to deal with the pain I encountered in my legs. He suggested that when I felt pain in my legs, I should mentally find the pain. When I did so, the pain moved. If, for example, I sought and located the pain in my knee, when I focused on it, it would move to my ankle. After several experiences with this, I soon discovered that my pain and the tension causing it were merely illusions, a mental obstruction created to prevent myself from sitting in meditation. My mind, which found sitting in meditation foreign to my experience, simply created reasons not to sit. But after a period of time during which I confronted the pain and discovered its unrealness, the pain vanished. Sitting was no longer foreign to my physical experience.

This same technique works well with the elimination of stress. Stress we might say is a total illusion as well; it is a self-inflicted mental response that creates physical ailments. When we learn to observe our habitual stress responses to life's experiences, many of the effects of stress will simply disappear.

By now it is clear that eliminating stress has little to do with methods that only allow you to avoid or hide from it. Like any other difficulty or destructive habit, stress needs to be dealt with in a hands-on manner. Taking vacations, ingesting drugs, or employing some other means of avoidance of stress will achieve only minor, temporary relief.

To eliminate stress you need to take a more direct, concrete approach, and that is dealing with yourself, since, as stated, the majority of stress responses are self-induced. The remedy is mimicking not the nervous, fragile little poodle, but the cat who is relaxed yet alert. One effective means of working on the self and achieving the ideal condition of the cat is self-massage. The different methods of self-massage, explained in detail in the following chapter, accomplish three things: first, they increase blood circulation; second, they relieve tension in the muscles; and third, they teach you to be mentally alert, attentive, and sensitive to stress. Hence, you learn how to both cure and eliminate existing stress and prevent it in the future.

Stress causes poor blood circulation, disruption of the central nervous system, and tension in the muscles. Massage, a primary method of increasing the circulation of the body's fluids and the suppleness of the muscles, is an effective technique for ridding the body of stress. The techniques of self-massage presented in the following chapter focus on the three main areas where symptoms of stress usually appear, namely the face, neck, and feet.

Stress appears in the face as a grimace, frown, or weary expression. Stress expresses itself in the neck as headaches, muscle pain, or loss of balance. Stress does not necessarily appear in the feet, but they are an area where the relief of stress can be successfully achieved. Asians have long known that attending to the feet benefits the entire body. Although a long discourse on reflexology, *qi* meridians, and the nervous system is beyond the scope of this book, suffice it to say they all find their foundation in the soles of the feet.

4

The Methods of Massaging Stress Away

SELF-MASSAGE THERAPY

Whenever you perform self-massage it is important to first rub your hands together vigorously to warm them. This in itself can be very healing to the skin and calm the nerves. It will also help stimulate blood flow into the hands.

It is best if these exercises are performed in a seated position on the edge of a chair; sit with your back straight and head held upright.

When reading the instructions below you will find that most of the movements are to be repeated thirty-six or forty-nine times. These numbers accord with the Chinese theory of yin and yang, and, although they need not be strictly adhered to, doing so will ensure that you perform an adequate number of motions for maximum effectiveness.

These massage techniques are effective not so much owing to the actual physical rubbing as to the stimulation of the *qi* meridians. These meridians are in function like a combination of blood vessels and nerve tissue; as *qi* flows through them, it behaves in a manner similar to that of nerve impulses. Stimulating a *qi* point on the body causes the *qi* to flow more freely. When *qi* meridians function properly the organs and central nervous system also function properly. According to Chinese medicine, the human body has three networks that connect all parts of the body: the blood system, through which blood and hormones travel; the nervous system, through which all sensory data travel; and the meridians, through which the *qi* travels. Chinese medical wisdom maintains that a person can survive a short time even after blood or nerve impulses cease, but a stop of the flow of *qi* results in immediate death. As stated earlier, *qi* is what animates the human body; everything else is simply a function of that animation.

So when pressing or rubbing on a certain point on the body, you are in fact affecting all three of these networks. Pressing stimulates blood flow and the release of healing hormones; it stimulates the nervous system to function properly; and finally it excites the *qi* and thus prevents it from becoming stagnant or blocked.

To get a good illustration of the effect of *qi* in your body, try the following simple exercise, one you may have done as a child. Stand in an open doorway and press your hands and arms really hard into the door frame. Press for about ten seconds, then release the pressure and step away. Notice that when you relax the pressure and step forward, your arms immediately float upward. This happens because a combination of blood and *qi* are rushing back into your arms; it has nothing to do with muscular activity. The natural flow of *qi,* so clearly demonstrated in this exercise, is the secret to the ability of the martial artist to react spontaneously and effortlessly to an attack, and it is the secret to achieving perfect health.

THE FACE METHODS

After warming the hands by rubbing the palms together vigorously (at least eighteen back and forth motions), place the palms over the face and eyes, and hold them there for approximately a minute; breathe gently. Follow the breathing patterns of breathing low in the abdomen as described in part 3 of the book and just let the warmth of your hands be absorbed by your face and eyes.

Self-massaging the face contains seven specific exercises:

1. MASSAGING THE FACE

Move the hands lightly in a circular motion over the entire facial area and forehead. The circular movement should be performed so that the hands move up and then outward, then down and inward and back to the starting position. Do this thirty-six times.

Massaging the Face

2. MASSAGING THE TEMPLES

Place the butt of the palms lightly over the temples and rub circularly thirty-six times.

Massaging the Temples

3. MASSAGING THE CHEEKS

Place the pads of the little fingers alongside the nose just below the eyes and the remaining fingers and the palms over the cheeks. Move both hands in small circular motions thirty-six times, paying special attention to the circular movements of the tips of the little fingers.

Massaging the Cheeks

4. MASSAGING THE MOUTH

Place the right hand over the mouth with the thumb pressed firmly against the right nostril so that the air is closed off. Move the hand in a clockwise circle thirty-six times keeping your thumb pressed against the right nostril and breathing through the left. Inhale every other circle, for a total of eighteen full breaths. Repeat using the left hand, but circle counterclockwise—this time with the thumb against the left nostril while you breathe from the right.

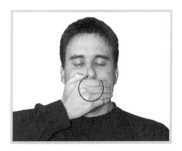

Massaging the Mouth

5. Massaging the Nose

Place the fingers of both hands alongside the nose and over the eyes, then pull and stretch the skin outward, then push inward and up, repeating these back and forth movements of the hands thirty-six times.

Massaging the Nose

6. Massaging the Skin

Using the fingertips of both hands, tap gently all over the face at least forty-nine times.

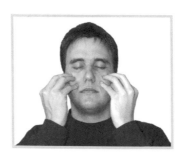

Massaging the Skin

7. Massaging the ears

Place the palms directly over the ears and, making sure to keep the head upright, rub circularly thirty-six times.

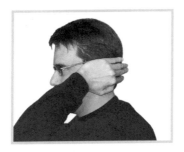

Massaging the Ears

The Neck Method

To massage the neck, simply place one hand on the back of the neck and rub back and forth thirty-six times. Perform the same movements with the other hand.

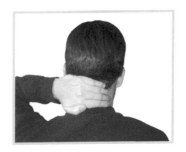 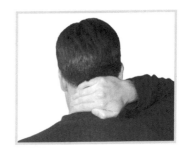

Massaging the Neck

THE FEET METHOD

Bring one foot up onto the opposite leg and massage the center of the arch of the foot, between the ball and heel, circularly thirty-six times. Next, grasp all the toes, with the thumb resting on the base of the big toe and the fingers curled around the remaining toes, and pull the toes back and forth thirty-six times. Last, pull on each toe, causing it to crack if possible. Repeat all three actions with the other foot.

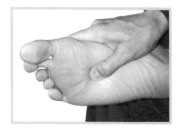 

Massaging the Feet

ACUPRESSURE TOUCH THERAPY

If you are new to acupressure, or if you are experiencing acute pain, use firm pressure. If, however, you are accustomed to acupressure, or have a chronic pain, then use hard pressure.

When pressing on a point, always accompany the pressure with small circular motions. Press and rub the area for no less than three minutes each session.

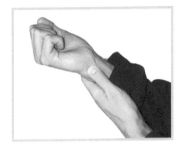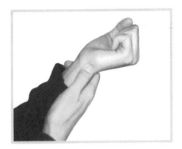

The Point for Anxiety and Nervousness

THE ACUPRESSURE POINT FOR ANXIETY AND NERVOUSNESS

This point (*shen man* in Chinese) is located on the distal crease of the wrist just below the butt of the palm on the baby finger side of the hand. Use the thumb to press and rub this point.

THE ACUPRESSURE POINT FOR HEADACHES

This point *(ho ku)* is located in the fleshy area between the index finger and thumb. Use the thumb of the opposite hand to press and rub this point.

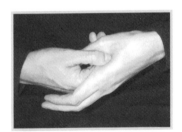

The Point for Anxiety and Headaches

The Acupressure Point
for Lowering Blood Pressure

This point *(jan chung)* lies at the center of the area between the nose and upper lip. Use the index finger to press and rub this point.

The Point for Lowering Blood Pressure

THE THIRD PATH

BREATHING STRESS AWAY

5

The Theory of Breathing Stress Away

About three thousand years ago the Chinese discovered that if a person focused on an area of pain in the body, breathed in through the nose, held the breath for a few seconds until a warmness could be felt in the afflicted area, and then exhaled while visualizing the pain departing from the area, the pain could be eliminated.

All Chinese natural healing methods derive from this simple exercise in concentration, breathing, and visualizing.

As stated previously, *qi* refers to both breath and what is called vital energy. According to Taoism, a person consists of physical energy and biological matter *(ching),* breath and vital energy *(qi),* and consciousness and spirit *(shen)*. In order to fully function as a human being, a person needs all three, and each affects the other. Thus, if the mind *(shen)* is tense, either the body *(ching)* or breath *(qi)* can calm it, and so on with each of the others.

Taoists were great observers of the human condition, and one of the things they perceived was how people's breathing patterns change throughout their lives. As infants we breathe low in our abdomens, but as we age our breath gradually rises to our chests. If we are fortunate enough to die a natural death, our last breath will be from the throat.

Based on their observations, Taoists believed that keeping the breath low in the abdomen throughout life was the secret to maintaining good health. Indeed, such breathing enhances blood circulation and suppleness of the body, and it induces a more tranquil state of mind.

Some people might argue that deep abdominal breathing negates or prevents proper cardiovascular functioning, but this is not true. Unlike the shallow, agitated chest breathing associated with aerobic exercise—which can sometimes lead to heart palpitations—abdominal breathing through the nose fully expands the lungs with filtered air and allows the breath to attain its highest potential of giving and maintaining health. There is also a common misperception that abdominal breathing means air is brought into the lower abdomen by literally inhaling as much of it as possible. Such a practice is ineffectual and induces a manner of breathing that is not beneficial to health.

Correct deep breathing might feel strange at first, but once you try it, you will begin to understand how effective it is. The first step is simply putting your attention on your lower abdomen. Try to sense what is going on there; feel and be attentive to the area. If you do so, almost immediately you will feel your breath there. This happens because the mind, as it ought, leads the breath, and the breath in turn leads the body. This is in fact the premise of all the martial arts developed in China. The process for eliminating stress is the same.

A few years ago when I was teaching a breathing class to a group of senior citizens, one of the ladies told me that she suffered from high blood pressure and had an appointment with her doctor the next morning. She was apprehensive about seeing him because she was concerned about the medication he wanted her to start taking. At the next class, however, three weeks later, she happily told me that when she was having her blood pressure checked, the doctor was amazed because she tested in the normal range. He asked her to come back in two weeks to have it checked again. Sure enough, her pressure was still normal, and so she avoided any need for medication.

She credited her improved health with what she learned in class, telling me that all she did was pay attention to her lower abdomen for fifteen minutes every morning and evening, and while having her pressure checked. She herself couldn't believe that something so simple could be so effective. She explained to her doctor what she was practicing, and he told her to keep it up. He confided that he himself practiced qigong (Chinese breathing and bodywork exercises) and hoped that more and more medical clinics and hospitals would incorporate these methods into their therapy practices.

The Methods of Breathing Stress Away

There are two primary methods for effectively breathing stress out of the body: *abdominal* and *heng ha* breathing. Both methods can be done in either a supine or seated position, as long as the back is kept straight and comfortable.

ABDOMINAL BREATHING

This method might at first seem strange because it appears to oppose what you may have read in the popular books on meditation and qigong exercises that exist today.

The primary benefit and purpose of this method is to create relaxation in the body and mind.

The technique is really quite simple as it calls only for paying attention to the lower abdomen. When doing so, you will feel the breath immediately in the lower abdomen. Breathing deeply, fully, and long, as most popular books instruct us to do, is unnatural, as it puts us in the position of forcing the breath to do something it is not prepared to do. The result of trying to breathe deeply will be nothing more than tiring quickly.

All you need do in this method is to breathe in and out through your nose, while keeping the mouth closed and putting all your attention on the lower abdomen, sensing, feeling, observing what is going on there, and nothing more. Just keep your attention and visualization on the lower abdomen; attempt to put your mind right there.

Do this for at least five minutes.

HENG HA BREATHING

Heng Ha breathing is a sort of inner listening to the sound of your breathing, although the breath should not be audible—it makes no external sound. It is a sensing of the expansion and contraction of the lungs, of the vibrations in the lower abdomen.

The primary benefit and purpose of this method of breathing is to expel stress from the body and mind. *Heng* is the natural sound of the inhalation, and it is what you listen for and focus on internally while inhaling. *Ha* is how the exhalation sounds naturally, and it is what you hear internally while exhaling.

In this breathing method, the inhalation is shorter than the exhalation. The inhalation is performed through the nose; the exhalation through the mouth. Let the exhalation fully expel before inhaling again. When exhaling in this manner, imagine that all your stress is being expelled and drained out through the mouth.

Again, perform this method of breathing for no less than five minutes each session.

7

Supplemental Breathing and Meditation Instructions

MENTAL CONCENTRATION

The most essential principle in meditation is to concentrate the mind and draw your attention to the lower abdomen. Successfully achieving this is difficult because our thoughts tend to wander. The end of one thought is but the beginning of another, flowing without end. Taoists say thoughts are like horses—they run wild and jump from one place to another.

The immediate goal of meditation is to fully subdue thoughts. When all wandering thoughts have subsided, you will experience a state of tranquillity.

If, in the beginning stages of meditation practice, wandering thoughts arise, attempt to settle them down by simply bringing yourself mentally back to the method. Practice this repeatedly and consistently. Over time wandering thoughts will naturally and gradually diminish, and a tranquil mind will result.

While sitting, close both eyes so that only a fine line of light can enter and you see the tip of the nose. Next, calmly and quietly breathe very naturally through the nose until you reach a state where no sound or sensation of breathing is experienced. Most important, keep your mental concentration on your lower abdomen.

The mouth should be comfortably closed. In the event that too much saliva is produced during meditation, carefully swallow it. Saliva is not a body excrement, rather a nourishing fluid, and it can have a great effect on breaking down gastric toxins that collect in the stomach.

With the eyes lightly closed, begin counting the breaths. One inhalation and one exhalation are counted as a complete breath. Continue counting until reaching ten complete breaths, then start over at one and repeat again and again.

Beginning practitioners of meditation encounter two kinds of obstacles in their practice. The first is confusion, which is simply having too many wandering and distracting thoughts. There is no fixed solution to this psychological state other than to keep returning to the method. The second is dullness. From time to time you will become drowsy, and the only cure is, again, to return to the practice by bringing yourself back to counting the breaths and focusing on the lower abdomen. Only through constant practice, of either long or short meditation periods, can wandering thoughts and the effects of dullness be reduced.

Training the Breath

The average person breathes very short, shallow breaths. High, shallow breathing prevents the full use of the lungs and results in the dissipation of all vitality. When the lungs are not fully used, an insufficient amount of air is inhaled, which in turn limits the discharge of the carbon dioxide in the blood, thus making the blood impure and the body vulnerable to illness.

The following five tips provide the correct procedures for inhaling and exhaling:

1. Breathe in and out delicately so that even you cannot hear the sounds of your breath moving in and out.
2. Don't hurry or force your breath. Just make use of the lower abdomen, and you will achieve success. The

most important thing is to breathe in a natural manner, without force or awkwardness.

3. Breathe diaphragmatically. Beginners often sense an agitation in the chest. This is the result of not exercising the diaphragmatic muscles. The procedure for exercising this muscle is as follows: When inhaling, breathe through the nose. This will stretch the base of the lungs and the lower portion of the diaphragmatic muscle. When exhaling, expel all the air by contracting the lower abdomen. This will exercise the upper portions of the diaphragm.

4. The abdominal region holds both the large and small intestines. They are extremely soft and pliable and can easily obstruct and hinder blood circulation. By taking in long, deep, and gradual breaths and making long, gradual exhalations—achieved by paying attention to the lower abdomen and not by trying to force the breath—you will gradually feel the breath in the lower abdomen and make the intestinal area more elastic. The obstructions in the abdomen can thus be fully corrected and controlled, placing everything in balance so that the blood can circulate freely and penetrate into the arms and legs.

5. Inhale and exhale through the nostrils. Do not use the mouth; the natural work of the nose is to breathe, to take in and expel air. The nostrils have many hairs that filter the mixture of microbes and dust that enter the nose, thus preventing them from entering the lungs. Unnaturally inhaling through the mouth wastes the important filtering function of the nose and allows dust and germs into the lungs, which can lead to illness and disease. Therefore, it is important to close the mouth while breathing, and not just during meditation.

Posturing the Body

Following are the standard Taoist body postures used in meditation. These are, according to Taoist teachings, the body positions most conducive to both regulating the breath and stimulating *qi* movement within the body.

Full Lotus Posture

To assume this posture, put the left foot on the right thigh, with the sole facing upward, then place the right foot on the left thigh, again with the sole facing up. It is important that the knees touch the sitting surface and that the upper body be erect, leaning neither to the front, back, left nor right.

Full Lotus Posture

Young people, with their relatively flexible, pliant muscles, usually have little difficulty assuming this posture, but it can be difficult for others, and it should not be forced. Rather, if you are having trouble, you should approach it gradually, holding the position until it can no longer be endured and then releasing the legs. Ideally, however, it is best to start with the half lotus or cross-legged postures before attempting the full lotus posture, so that the flexibility needed can be acquired comfortably.

HALF LOTUS POSTURE

Sit and place the left or right foot on the opposite thigh, sole facing upward. Next, place the other foot beneath the opposite leg to complete the posture. Although the half lotus posture is easier to assume than the full lotus posture, its shortcoming is that it can prevent the knee of the raised leg from directly touching the sitting surface, and,

Half Lotus Posture

after sitting in the posture for a while, the body might begin to lean slightly toward the side. Being aware of these potential problems and attempting to correct them when you can is all that is necessary; don't feel anxious about not being able to perfectly sit in the posture because the shortcomings are not a serious hindrance.

CROSS-LEGGED POSTURE

If both the half lotus and full lotus postures are uncomfortable for you, then start out in the cross-legged position, which involves sitting with one leg in front of the other, the soles of the feet facing upward and the knees touching the sitting surface. Keeping the knees pressed against the sitting surface may prove difficult, and you will be likely to lean. Pay

Cross-legged Posture

attention to your posture, however, and you will gradually correct these problems.

SITTING ON A CHAIR

If you cannot sit on the floor with your legs crossed in any of the three postures described above, then sitting normally on a chair will work. It is important, however, to sit erect near the edge of the seat, with the feet placed flat on the floor and hip width apart.

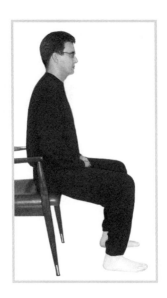

Sitting on a Chair

HAND POSITION

Both hands must be relaxed, without the least bit of tension exerted in effecting their position and placement. Place the back of the left hand lightly in the palm of the right hand, so that both palms are facing upward. Then set the hands on top of the upper thigh area so that the palms appear to be supporting the lower abdomen.

Hand Position

HEAD POSITION

For efficacious meditation, attention must be paid to the head, neck, face, eyes, and jaws. The head and neck should be held erect and upright, the face should be positioned directly to the front, the eyes closed lightly, the jaws closed just so there is no separation between them, and the tongue held gently against the palate.

SUPINE POSTURE

Practicing meditation in a supine position, even though physically easy, can result in heavy mental dullness. Nonetheless, if there is some inconvenience or you are unable to sit in an upright position, a supine posture should be employed as an alternative.

There are two styles of supine meditation: lying on the back and lying on the right side. Lying flat on the back is the common supine position. It is important to keep the head and neck aligned, facing directly upward, and the shoulders relaxed and touching the supporting surface. Use a thick cushion or mat, wear comfortable clothing, and always maintain self-awareness.

The other method here is to simply lie on your right side. Lying on the left side can produce a continual aching on the left side from the heart being constrained, so it should be

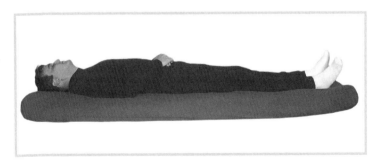

Lying on the Back

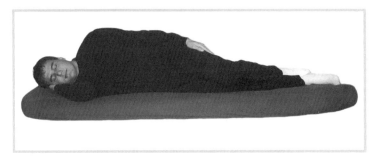

Lying on the Right Side

avoided, especially by those who suffer from heart problems or stress.

The attitude of the eyes, mouth, head, and so on is the same as explained above. The only difference is that in the second type of supine position, the head and body should be bent and bowed forward.

In the second type of supine position, the right leg is extended with only a slight bend at the knee, while the left leg is bent more and pushed slightly beyond the right; the calves of both legs touch lightly. The left arm is extended, with the palm resting gently on the thigh; the right palm is placed beneath the head like a pillow. It is important to periodically examine your posture and make any necessary corrections.

Comments on Breathing

The breath moves through different stages during meditation. Note that all stages, however, make use of the idea of mentally leading the breath. The first stage is simply counting the breath. This consists of counting only each exhalation. Count to ten exhalations and then start all over again, repeating this during the meditation time. If you become confused or distracted, just keep returning to counting from one again until you can count ten exhalations without obstruction during the entire sit. When using this method, constantly sense the breath and the counting in the lower abdomen. In this stage you can experience one-pointed concentration (no straying thoughts, just total focus on the breath), and the ordinary sense of time will disappear, so that an hour will feel like just a few minutes or less.

The next stage is to just sense the inhalation and exhalation in the lower abdomen. Simply be aware of each part of the breath, and always return to counting the breath if you become confused or distracted. It is in this stage that you can experience true breath, wherein the breath appears to be working of its own accord, with no physical effort required, and it seems incredibly full and active. It will also feel as though only a few breaths have been taken during the meditation time. There is also sometimes the sense of not wanting to get up when the sitting time is over. This should not concern you, as it means the body is starting to adjust to the tranquillity of sitting.

Afterword

I hope this book has been of some help to you in your quest for eliminating stress from your life.

The methods I have provided here are very effective if applied and performed daily. A famous Zen master once said, "There is no other secret to being successful at anything other than simple repetition of the method . . . repeat, repeat . . . that is all."

When you think about it, that is how you took upon your level of stress in the first place: you kept repeating the same stress-inducing thoughts and actions. So it is my hope that you make use of these methods and live stress free, and maybe even take them further to realize complete self-awareness.

About the Author

In 1979 and 1980, as a resident of Ju Lai Ssu monastery at the City of Ten-Thousand Buddhas in Talmage, California, Stuart Alve Olson began learning the Chinese language and studying Buddhist philosophy, taking formal refuge in Buddhism from Ch'an master Hsuan Hua. While there, he learned the Eight Brocades qigong practices from dharma master Chen Yi.

In 1982 the famous t'ai chi ch'uan master Tung-tsai Liang (presently 102 years old) invited Stuart to live and study with him at his home in St. Cloud, Minnesota. Stuart was the only student ever granted this honor. Stuart stayed in Master Liang's home for more than six years, studying both t'ai chi ch'uan and qigong practices, as well as the Chinese language, all under Master Liang's tutelage. Since then Stuart has traveled extensively throughout the United States with Master Liang, assisting him in his teaching. Stuart has also taught in

Canada, Hong Kong, and Indonesia and has traveled throughout Asia. In addition, he has studied massage in both Taiwan and Indonesia.

Stuart presently lives in northern California, where he writes about Asia-related subjects and teaches.

If you wish to contact him please send letters in care of the publisher or e-mail him through his Web site at www.taichi-web.com.

BOOKS OF RELATED INTEREST

Qigong Teachings of a Taoist Immortal
The Eight Essential Exercises of Master Li Ching-yun
by Stuart Alve Olson

The Jade Emperor's Mind Seal Classic
The Taoist Guide to Health, Longevity, and Immortality
by Stuart Alve Olson

T'ai Chi According to the I Ching
Embodying the Principles of the Book of Changes
by Stuart Alve Olson

Tai Chi for Kids
Move with the Animals
by Stuart Alve Olson
Illustrated by Gregory Crawford

Energy Balance through the Tao
Exercises for Cultivating Yin Energy
by Mantak Chia

Chi Self-Massage
The Taoist Way of Rejuvenation
by Mantak Chia

Transforming Your Dragons
How to Turn Fear Patterns into Personal Power
by José Stevens, Ph.D.

The Stress-Free Habit
*Powerful Techniques for Health and Longevity from the Andes,
Yucatan, and the Far East*
by John Perkins

Inner Traditions • Bear & Company
P.O. Box 388
Rochester, VT 05767
1-800-246-8648
www.InnerTraditions.com

Or contact your local bookseller